OUR WORLD IN COLOUR

BALI

OUR WORLD IN COLOUR

BALI

Photography by Ian Lloyd
Text by Patrick R. Booz

The Guidebook Company Limited

Reprinted 1992.

Distributors

Australia and New Zealand: The Book Company,
100 Old Pittwater Road, Brookvale, NSW 2100, Australia.

Canada: Prentice Hall Canada,
1870 Birchmount Road, Scarborough, Ontario MIP 257, Canada.

Hong Kong: China Guides Distribution Services Ltd.,
14 Ground Floor, Lower Kai Yuen Lane, North Point, Hong Kong.

India and Nepal: UBS Publishers' Distributors Ltd.,
5 Ansari Road, Post Box 7015, New Delhi 110 002, India.

Singapore and Malaysia: MPH Distributors (S) PTE Ltd.,
601 Sims Drive, No. 03/07-21, Pan-I Complex, Singapore 1438.

USA: Publishers Group West Inc.,
4065 Hollis, Emeryville, CA 94608, USA.

The publishers would like to thank Bill Dalton for permission to reproduce extracts from his *Indonesia Handbook* (Moon Publications) in the A-Z section

Photography by Ian Lloyd
Text and captions by Patrick R Booz
Edited by Nick Wallwork
Designed by Joan Law Design & Photography

Printed in China

ISBN: 962-217-111-7

Title spread
A lone temple was built on the shore of Lake Bratan to venerate the Goddess of the Waters. Rituals and celebrations take place here for the blessing of irrigation water, which flows from this high-altitude lake to nourish rice fields far below.

Right
Dawn comes up behind Lake Batur. This lake lies inside one of the world's largest volcanic basins, surrounded by a mountain rim that measures 13 kilometres (eight miles) across. In the centre is Gunung Batur, a holy volcano, second only in importance to Gunung Agung, mother-mountain of Bali. Batur's awesome power has been felt twice this century, and these eruptions finally forced the inhabitants to leave their villages by the lake and resettle high above on the mountain rim, safe from the gas, ashes and molten lava.

Pages 6-7
The temple of Tanah Lot stands out against a salmon-coloured sunset on the southwest coast of Bali. Situated on an isolated promontory, this is one of the island's important sea temples where the spirits and dwellers of the deep are honoured.

Pages 8-9
Hard work and year-round care are necessary to maintain these beautiful terraced rice fields. In the countryside, life's activities centre around rice, and villages, hidden away in groves of trees, are invariably close to the fields.

Pages 10-11
Children play in the golden light of Kuta Beach. Free and self-reliant at an early age, children are raised by a liberal hand at home and learn from nature in their games and in their daily forays to seashore, fields and mountain slopes.

Page 12-13
A colourful crowd, united in common devotion, comes to celebrate a temple festival. It is the odalan, the birthday of the temple's founding, and the whole village attends, dressed in finest clothing. The festivities, lasting for a day and a night, mark a fresh beginning for the temple year.

BALI SEA

Singaraja

Mt Batur

Lake Buyan

Lake Bratan

Mt Merbuk

Lake Batur

Mt Mesehe

Mt Patas

Mt Agung

Negara

Mt Seraya

Tabanan

Ubud

BADUNG STRAIT

Mas

Tanah Lot

Denpasar

Legian

Kuta

Sakenan Temple

Nusa Penida

BALI

INTRODUCTION

The island of Bali is just one of thousands of islands in the Malay Archipelago, that great chain that straddles the equator from New Guinea to the tip of Sumatra and once, eons ago, formed a land bridge between Asia and Australia. Yet unlike the other islands, Bali has held sway in the world's imagination for most of this century. Bali's special reputation came about for several reasons, but to the visitor its allure and fascination are clear and immediate. The island is physically beautiful and the people, lithe, graceful and full of friendliness, exude a quiet confidence.

To the Balinese, their island is the entire world. Other worlds may exist outside, but theirs is complete and whole in itself, a total provider, bountiful with all the physical and spiritual attributes important to existence. In fact the Balinese cosmos is so rich that the psychic, unseen world is constantly spilling over into the mundane. Daily life is a constant, vibrant expression of the need to honour, praise and propitiate gods and nymphs, demons and witches. Hardly a day goes by without a procession or temple festival, and at night villages far and wide come alive to opera and dance-drama, accompanied by the strange, hypnotic music of *gamelan* percussion orchestras. To an outsider, Balinese life seems to be a continuous celebration with brief intervals for rest.

According to legend, Bali originated as a special event during the creation of the universe. Through the purity of meditation the phenomenal world emerged, magnificently arrayed, layer upon layer, from the base of the cosmos below to the perfumed heavens above. In between, the island of Bali appeared, resting on an immense turtle afloat in a vast ocean.

The scientific explanation of the island's birth and development is a wonderful story as well. Once connected to the massive Asiatic mainland, Bali became an island after the melting of the polar ice caps nearly 120 million years ago. Bali is considered the last outpost of mainland Asia, separated by a 305-metre deep (1,000-foot) channel from the island of Lombok to the east. This channel also represents an ecological boundary known as the Wallace Line after the 19th-century naturalist Alfred Russell Wallace. He noted that Bali has luxurious tropical vegetation and animals such as elephants, tigers, monkeys and wild cattle, while Lombok and islands to the east suggest an affiliation with Australia and not Asia. Here, east of the Wallace Line, the climate is more arid and the vegetation thorny and scrub-like. The animals include primitive marsupials, the world's largest lizards, parrots and cockatoos and relatively few insect species.

Bali is just over 5,181 square kilometres (2,000 square miles) in area, barely one-quarter the size of Wales, and densely populated with nearly three million inhabitants. Its tropical richness and the ingenious use of terraced rice fields allow the land to support such overcrowding. Elaborate systems of irrigation bring water from the high volcanoes to the shimmering emerald-green fields found in most corners of the island. Rice is the most important food in Bali; the crop is the source of life and wealth and is recognized as a gift from the gods. Legend tells that rice first appeared on Bali when the male God of Water raped Mother Earth to beget rice. Wet-rice farming has existed on Bali for well over 1,000 years, and today's amazing, contoured landscape is the heritage of 50 generations of farmers.

The need to tend the rice and care for the fields led to the rise of the *desa*, or village, the chief social unit in Bali. It is much more than just a village, however; it is community, parish and focal point of all life for the Balinese. Cozy and safe within a lush grove, surrounded by walls and bountiful trees — coconut, banana, papaya, bread-fruit — the *desa* functions to maintain the cosmic balance and harmony within the area of its jurisdiction, thus assuring the well-being of all. Every *desa*, and

15

Portraits of Balinese men. In the tropical weather people dress for comfort and ease, though there are flourishes that add colour and style to each person's appearance. Men wear the udeng, *a square piece of cloth tied into a turban. Each man ties it in a different way, to create a distinctive, individual style.*

there are hundreds of them spread throughout the island, is thus seen to be fulfilling its obligation to gods and men.

Bali has often been called 'Land of the Many Temples'. Temples, from small shrines in the rice fields to magnificent complexes belonging to large towns, are certainly the single most important institution on the island, and they can be seen everywhere. By the sea, on desolate promontories, in caves, on the highest mountains, even entangled in the roots of banyan trees, large and small temples appear as a natural complement to the island's geography.

From earliest times, before the overwhelming influence of Hindu temple building arrived from Java a thousand years ago, there have been special places, plots of consecrated ground, where altars, cairns and stone enclosures marked a kind of primitive temple. Such temples still can be seen in the eastern part of the island where isolated villages protected these old forms.

Every Balinese community has at least three main temples: the foundation temple of the original village, often hundreds of years old, a town temple for communal celebrations, and the temple of the dead for the gods associated with death and cremation. The reason for this division is to maintain a sacred balance between the innumerable, contending forces of the invisible world, which to the Balinese has a trenchant reality.

It is difficult to know exactly how many large temples exist on Bali. An attempt to count them was once made after the devastating earthquake of 1917, when 2,431 temples were completely destroyed in one district. This district was moderately populated and comprised about one-ninth of the island's surface area. From this it was deduced that Bali had at least 20,000 important temples at the time, and today, if anything, the number has grown.

The language of Bali is of the Austronesian family, a vast and diverse group of languages that extends from Hawaii and Easter Island in the east to Taiwan, the islands of Indonesia and Madagascar in the west. Balinese is more closely related to the languages and dialects of its eastern neighbours than to Javanese, the tongue spoken to the west by nearly 80 million people. Nevertheless, Old Javanese and Sanskrit have greatly influenced Bali's vocabulary, much as Latin and French have contributed to English.

The outstanding characteristic of Balinese is the use of 'vocabularies of courtesy', a linguistic phenomenon that developed with the introduction of Hindu caste hierarchies. There are in fact three special vocabularies within the one main language. Common speech is used between friends and intimates and employed when speaking to a person of lower social standing. The polite form is spoken to strangers (before their rank is known) and to superiors. The deferential form is employed when speaking to high caste persons, priests and other important people. Misuse of these three vocabularies, whether through ignorance or arrogance, is a serious *faux pas*, and in certain extreme, but rare, cases could result in a court case and punishment.

In spite of these special vocabularies and the traditional, strict adherence to social rank through caste, daily interaction between people is remarkably frank and easygoing. There is a universal sense of happiness and gentleness among the Balinese, and their polite ways and deference are thoroughly natural and unaffected.

Art and ritual are the living breath of the Balinese. There have been times and places in the West, in Renaissance Florence for example, where people expected beauty in their surroundings, where they talked and gossiped about artists endlessly, and where they appreciated and demanded high artistic standards. Such ways have always been the way of the Balinese; nearly everyone, high or low, man or woman, young or old, is engaged and competent in an art or a craft. Technically speaking the words 'art' and 'artist' do not exist in the Balinese language, which is perhaps a reflection of the universal involvement of Balinese with some form of aesthetic expression. Although a great painter or carver is recognized as such, and given pride of place in the community, he or she is not part of a separate class of artists, but is instead no different from a farmer, clerk or simple labourer.

Hand in hand with this casual and self-effacing attitude towards talent, where the greatest good is simply to create something beautiful for the community, the temple or the gods, is the ephemerality of Balinese art. Tropical decay is constantly at work. Wooden posts and statues are the prey of insects, rain and humidity destroy paper and cloth, the sun and heat assure that lovingly made offerings of palm fronds, fruit and flowers last only a day. Even stone carvings have a relatively short life. Sandstone and lava, soft and friable, are the only materials available and, after a few years, the friezes and intricate sculptures into which they have been shaped become unrecognizable. There is a constant need to recreate, replace and rebuild, which makes for the freshness and everlasting youth of Balinese art.

A carved dancer forms part of a temple relief.

The Balinese look back proudly to a glorious past of rajas, princes and heroines, times that brought them their traditions and laid the foundations for a remarkable, vibrant society. Confident in their origins and world view, they have never suffered from stagnation, and their very openness to influences beyond their world has helped to create a special, eclectic mind and aesthetic. Absorption, adaptation and flux have always been a part of Balinese life, an ongoing source of creativity. Influences from Southeast Asia, India, Java, China, Europe, and now even Australia and America, have touched Bali to greater or lesser degrees, leaving their imprint on the people and the art, but they always are transformed in a uniquely Balinese way, with zest, vigour, colour and, frequently, humour. Where else but in Bali could you have an outrageous painting of anthropomorphic frogs snapping away with their cameras? Or a new wall carving on a 16th-century temple showing fat Dutchmen in an automobile?

The powerful and dreaded Rangda, widow-witch and queen of evil spirits, stands at a temple entrance.

Amidst the playfulness is a deeper, darker side to Balinese life. In various forms of expression, but usually in that of the dance-drama, the Balinese express the deepest concerns of their collective unconscious. These have to do with struggles between good and evil, strong and weak, clean and unclean.

Dance and drama are a united form in Bali and do not occupy separate spheres as in the West. They grew out of a religious tradition and in most cases still have religious importance. Entertainment of the deity with dance and music is as natural to the Balinese as the presentation of offerings.

Dance in Bali also brings delight to the people and fulfills many needs and purposes. The *baris* dance, for example, is full of martial expression and gives vent to manly virtues and preoccupations. The *legong*, probably Bali's finest dance, is highly refined and feminine and appreciated on a purely aesthetic level. The *kebyar* is a solo performance of brilliant showmanship. Fun and flirtation are the soul of the *joged* and *janger*, and a wide range of historical and mythic epics find expression in the *topeng* masked dramas and *wayang* shadow puppet plays.

Dances that involve trance, however, lie at the core of the Balinese. Here contact is made with the unseen, and fragile humans become heroic as they enter into the world beyond. In the dance called *sangyang*, young girls bring luck and protective magic to the temple and village. They are the psychic adventurers who go over to the other side to bring back news of the gods, to convey their wishes and moods. Even death itself is approached. As intermediaries and confidants of the deities, they return and help bind together the community by sharing the experience of their contact. They reassure everyone by showing that awesome, unknown mysteries can be faced and survived.

Painted stone carving of a priest holding his sacred bell.

17

An animal offering, with scarf around its neck, arrives for the start of a purification ceremony. Mirrors, banners and painted, tooled leather adorn a bull in north Bali. Bull races highlight the festival which is held to prepare the fields before planting new rice.

Every young dancer is rigorously trained under the care of a special teacher, himself more than likely a once-famous performer. But the hidden stresses and unpredictability of trance dancing sometimes erupt into wild and frenzied displays that abandon all discipline and only permit order once exhaustion overtakes the dancers. In times of turmoil, some villages will hold trance dances night after night to keep the land calm. Expression of the deities' will, in whatever form, is seen to be a purgative and a balm.

The uses of trance can serve other ends as well. It might be 'discovered' through a trance intermediary that the god in one village is the mother of a god in another. A procession of visitation must take place, and, intentionally or not, two places are brought closer together, old feuds set aside. Trance can also legitimate political movements by revealing the 'correctness' of a particular ideology, and it sometimes explains new developments or strange occurrences, such as natural calamities, that confound a community.

The most powerful use of trance, and the most magically dangerous dance-drama, takes the form of a titanic struggle between the forces of good and evil. Nothing short of humanity's welfare is at stake.

This is the symbolic play of Barong and Rangda, Bali's two most remarkable creatures. The Barong is a benevolent, mystical beast, Lord of the Forest, who intercedes on behalf of mankind to fight disease, black magic and all forms of pollution. His adversary is the hideous Rangda, witch-widow, child-eater and Queen of Death. Barong enters first, dancing and prancing, played by two men hidden beneath a holy mask and lion's body. Rangda then appears with a terrifying fanged mask, its flaming tongue hanging far down between two grotesque pendulous breasts. Fighting begins and the course of battle shifts from side to side. At the moment Rangda appears to win, a group of men, all entranced and wielding daggers, rush to Barong's aid. Rangda's witchcraft turns the men's blades against themselves in the fearful climax of the drama. These men in a cataleptic state engage in self-torture, and only the Barong's power saves them. There is no decisive resolution to this dance-drama — only a temporary victory for the forces of good and a short-lived abeyance of wickedness. Everyone goes home exhausted and relieved, knowing there will be more music and drama, more exuberance and excitement in the days to come.

Recognition of Bali's special place in world culture arrived slowly. In the 16th century Europe's great powers came to the East Indies in search of spices and colonial footholds. Portugal and Spain were first, followed soon after by Britain and Holland. There were certainly sightings of Bali by these foreigners, and even a landing in 1580 by the irrepressible Sir Francis Drake, but no written records of Bali were made until the final years of the 16th century. In 1597 a Dutch party came ashore and wrote the first detailed, though superficial, description of the island. For the next one-and-a-half centuries knowledge of Bali remained scant, with only occasional visits and commentaries by outsiders. In the mid-19th century things changed with the arrival of a profound Sanskrit scholar. That marked the beginning of serious study of Balinese culture, and there followed a string of excellent, dedicated Dutch academics who have continued their work up to the present day.

But the great age of Bali's blossoming, its 'opening' to the world, was in the 1930s. It was then that a small, influential group of Western artists, anthropologists, ethnomusicologists and novelists produced an outstanding body of work, sensitive and full of insight into Balinese life. Unfortunately among general readers the idea of Bali as Paradise developed, and this misreading was exacerbated by tour operators and cruise ships that brought tourists by the hundreds to gawp at bare-breasted maidens and take snapshots of 'temple dancers'. In addition, at about the same time, a series of sensationalist films on Bali became popular in Europe and North America. *Goona-goona* was the title of one of these films. It means 'magic' in Balinese, but became a slang term in New York for sex appeal.

As early as 1937 the writer Miguel Covarrubias, a keen observer and advocate of Balinese culture, predicted gloomily that the way of life 'is doomed to disappear under the merciless onslaught of modern commercialism and standardization'. Fifty years on, the question remains: 'Is Balinese culture already ruined or will it be able to withstand the onslaught of tourism?'. In some respects the question is moot, as such issues, vitally important to the Balinese, can only be answered by the local people themselves. For all the exotic characteristics of Balinese culture, it has one enduring and fundamental goal: balance and harmony within the natural and supernatural worlds. If the people of Bali can hold fast to this goal, no external force can defeat their spirit or way of life.

The real Bali does still exist, though the quality of this reality varies from place to place. The finest and truest the island has to offer will not appear effortlessly to the casual observer, though patience, care and understanding can help reveal Bali's magic. The pictures in this book are an affirmation, and their force and colour a small souvenir of a beautiful island.

An entrance tower guards the way to the royal palace of Puri Agung at Karengasem, east Bali. This was the site of the island's most important state in the late 18th and early 19th centuries. The tower and palace buildings are excellent examples of indigenous and imported architectural styles.

Following page
At Batuan, the famous cultural centre of central Bali, a procession winds its way through the paddy fields. These dancers form a gambuh *troupe; they perform one of the oldest dance-dramas on the island. It depicts chivalrous heroes and historical episodes from Bali's mythical past.*

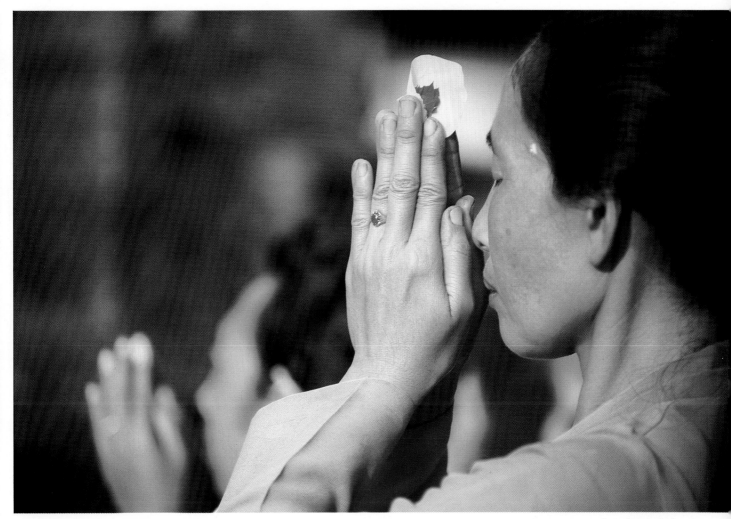

Preceding page
Warriors and brutish attendants march across a painted panel at the Hall of Justice, Klungkung. Vivid ceiling paintings show scenes from Heaven and Hell, symbolic of the rewards and punishments awaiting defendants. This was the highest court in the land during the 18th century.

In a moment of single-minded prayer, a woman presents a flower offering. As a gift to the gods, offerings must be pleasing but they can be as simple as a petal or a few grains of rice on a banana leaf. Each day of the week has its special spiritual attributes, and these determine what type, colour and form each offering should take.

Water from the jungly mountains streams through a temple complex of pagodas and pavilions. Channeled water and pools have always been a part of sacred sites, for purposes of washing and ritual cleansing.

Women wash clothes in the morning light of Lake Bratan, one of three lakes within a huge volcanic basin. Bali boasts four great volcanoes that stretch in a jumble from west to east, culminating in Gunung Agung, (right), the island's tallest and holiest.

Besakih Temple lies under the shadow of Gunung Agung at an altitude of 950 metres (3,000 feet). It represents the most sacred point of the compass for Balinese and has been a royal ancestral sanctuary since earliest times. Even the names of the gods enshrined here exist only in Old Balinese, predating influences from India or Java.

A girl of Ubud rests near a newly transplanted field of rice.

Harvesting rice is hard work, but the labour is done with happiness and a sense of anticipation of the coming festivals to celebrate the end of the rice cycle. In Bali three words for rice are used: padi, *origin of the English term* paddy, *indicates rice still in the field;* beras *means threshed rice; and* nasi *is the final form of the cooked, edible grain.*

Emerald fields of rice run through hills and valleys to the abrupt slopes of Gunung Batukau, a volcano that rises to 2,276 metres (7,467 feet). All parts of Bali that use irrigation are divided into units, and each of these local territories has its own temple and village organization to look after it.

Right
An 11-tiered meru tower rises above the forest. These pagoda-like structures, a common feature of temple architecture, must have an odd number of storeys to fulfill their magical function of protection. Merus are symbolically associated with Gunung Agung, Mountain of the Gods. The little roofs are made of sugar-palm fibre and are sometimes covered with corrugated iron.

A woman uses the evening breeze to help winnow rice.

A temple courtyard is used as a threshing ground. Once individual grains of rice have been separated from the ear they are swept up and bagged; they are then ready for sale or distribution before the final process of husking and polishing.

*The witch-widow Rangda,
Goddess of Death and Queen of
Evil Spirits, is seen in many
forms on Bali: in paintings, in
the dance-drama and, as here, in
temple statuary. She represents
the forces of darkness and
harms the world with her black
magic. Long fangs, bulging eyes
and fiery tongue hanging
between ugly, hairy breasts
make her fearful, and
youngsters especially are
terrified by her reputation as a
bloodthirsty child-eater.*

Right
*Three boys are safe in the
doorway of a temple. The
monumental gate is raised high
on stone platforms and leads
into the courtyard of the temple
proper. The deity above the door
appears malevolent, but he is in
fact a protector and will hurt
only those who enter with evil
intentions.*

Following page
*Intricate, gaudy offerings called
tjilis are made of moulded, fried
rice flour, dyed with brilliant
colours and embellished with
flowers.*

Above
A group of women shares a joke while working together to make temple offerings. This is a time to gossip and relax while doing something useful for the community. Stripped palm fronds will be folded and pinned to create lamaks, pretty, perishable decorations (right) that usually only last one day before becoming wilted and spent.

Left and far right
Sometimes detailed, other times stylized and made of simple palm leaves (page 38), tjilis represent beautiful girls with slender bodies and large headdresses. Their origins can be traced back to primitive rites that honoured the deities of rice and fertility.

Solemnity marks the beginning of the Tooth Filing Ceremony, usually conducted when the young approach puberty. A priest leads the ceremony, and at its climax the initiates lie down and have their teeth filed into neat, clean rows. This is a symbolic purification. By removing all points and rough edges of the teeth, the filing ritually overcomes the base characteristics of greed, sloth, hatred and ignorance, preparing the youngster to take part in the full life of the community.

A temple festival takes place at Bangli. This temple, Pura Kehan, has a history of 800 years and is a fine example of the southern style of architecture. It is built of reddish-pink brick and has intricate carvings in grey and pink sandstone.

A huge procession forms part of the odalan, *a celebration to mark the village temple's anniversary. Days of preparation go into a successful* odalan *and the culmination is this march to the sea where statues of the temple gods will be given a ritual bath. Women (above) with waists wrapped in beautiful saffron scarves carry offerings of cloth, flowers, fruit and holy water. Gongs and orchestral music accompany the general noise and gaiety of the crowd.*

*A concerned onlooker watches
as a group of young men lose
control in a state of trance.
Friends and caretakers of the
trance ceremony keep them
from hurting themselves or
people in the crowd. Trance is
not at all unusual in Bali; it is
encouraged as a special state in
which people can enter into
direct communication with the
spirit world and bring back
knowledge or special wishes of
the deities. Even in moments of
ecstasy or self-inflicted violence,
trance is rarely allowed to get
out of control.*

On foot and in overloaded boats, crowds of people head off for a festival at the temple of Pura Sakenan, a holy site for the people of southern Bali. It sits on the shore of Serangan, better known as Turtle Island for its huge sea turtles. These are especially prized as food for village feasts.

Following page
Tall banners stand before the temple of Tanah Lot. This small, beautifully located temple was built in the 16th century by Sang Hiyang Nirartha, the last important priest to come to Bali from Java. He arrived to strengthen the island's Hindu faith, and Tanah Lot is a memorial to his efforts.

Cremations are one of the typically Hindu phenomena of Bali. Seen more as a celebration than a time of mourning, a cremation is a social event where families can gain prestige by displaying extravagance in fulfilling a final, sacred duty. Tower-like structures called *bade* hold the body while it is taken to the cremation site. *Bades* represent the cosmos — underworld, earth, heaven — while the multiple roofs are replicas of the levels of heaven. Bulls and leonine creatures are the most common form of sarcophagi, the last resting place before the soul is purified and released by the fires of cremation.

A Brahmanic priest is employed to oversee the whole affair, from choosing a propitious day for the funeral to conducting the many proper rituals for the dead.

Following page
Two boats with outriggers, looking like giant water-striders, rest on the shore of Lake Batur.

Preceding page
Balinese masks are carved realistically, full of human feeling and expressiveness. A good set of masks is a treasure for the community lucky enough to own it. The most famous mask-dance is the topeng, *which means literally 'something pressed against the face'.*

Shadow puppets, seen in profile and projected onto a screen by the light of an oil lamp, are made of thinly cut buffalo skin, painted and gilded to wonderful effect. Known as wayang kulit, *stage performances of these shadow puppets are the main medium for classical poetry and epic history, all important in the spiritual education of the common people.*

A young baris *dancer strikes a martial pose. The* baris *is a ritual war dance, stately and full of pomp. It is an expression of manly attributes and was the precursor of all male dances on Bali. Performers must be fit as all parts of the body, from the forehead to the toes, are used in action. Music always accompanies the* baris, *and the relation of dance to music is close, with many changes of mood and expression.*

Two girls dance with all the skill and concentration they possess. Dance training begins at an early age and requires years of rigorous training. At first, a teacher guides the girls through the movements, leading them by the wrists again and again until the entire choreography is an indelible part of them.

A young Legong dancer.

The dance-pantomime known as legong *is the best loved of classical dances in Bali. Only girls perform the* legong, *often beginning their training at age five. By 14 they are too old and retire forever from this style of dancing. The girls are called 'divine nymphs' and act the roles of highly refined courtiers.*

Janger *dancers with remarkable florid head-dresses move across a temple courtyard. The dance began around 1925 and was strongly influenced by Malay opera. It was also the first social dance in Bali where boys and girls could join together and have fun. The* janger *had a brief and glorious period, epitomizing the Balinese love of new things, but today it is performed mostly for tourists.*

Following page
The kecak *is a dance with large groups of men singing, chanting and moving together with the music. The best known* kecak *accompanies stories from the Ramayana, the great Hindu epic, and trance dancing is frequently an element of these performances. It is also known as the Monkey Dance, named for an episode where the male chorus plays a jabbering band of monkeys in thrall of its leader, Hanuman, the Monkey King.*

The gamelan, *a percussion orchestra made up primarily of metallophones, numerous suspended gongs and many types of cymbals, is an indispensable part of Balinese creative life. Most villages have one or two gamelan orchestras, and the strange music with its subtle beauty can be heard throughout the island nearly every evening. The bamboo flute (right) is used as a lead for the melody.*

Bali's most powerful drama revolves around the confrontation and clash of two mythical creatures, Barong and Rangda, *personifications of the forces of good and evil. The Barong (left) is a lion-beast that represents sunshine, medicine, life and light. Despite his fierce look he is the antidote for evil and he likes to dance for the sheer joy of entertainment.*

But Barong's playfulness is interrupted by the appearance of Rangda, hideous witch and Queen of Death. In the climactic struggle that ensues, trance dancers rush to Barongs aid, only to have their daggers turned against themselves by Rangda's evil magic (right). Barong's own power prevents the daggers from piercing flesh no matter how the entranced men try to kill themselves. In the end the dancers are slowly brought out of trance with the aid of Barong's beard, his centre of power. There is no ultimate winner in the cosmic struggle; goodness gains only a temporary victory and evil invariably engages in the battle again.

Every third day is a major market day on Bali. Traditionally, women control the goods and do nearly all the buying and selling. They stream into towns in the morning and by noon the activity is at its height, the marketplace filled with exotic smells of pepper, cinnamon, mace, coconut oil, dried fish and fried sweetbreads. Two women (above) relax at the end of a market day.

Bali, covering just over 2,000 square miles in area, has a population of nearly three million inhabitants. The Balinese people are known for their gentleness, humour and creativity.

A mask-maker from Mas shows off one of his works. In former times the famous artists of this region worked solely for the temples and royal courts. Nowadays secular art is widespread and masks can be made for pleasure and sold commercially

An artist emerges from behind two panels of his forest painting. Painting in Bali went through a period of rejuvenation in the 1930s when it was strongly influenced and encouraged by European artists. They introduced new materials, themes and treatment of light and helped liberate painting from static, traditional forms.

For more than 50 years tourists have been coming to Bali to play, to relax, to learn and to share in the special magic of the island. A family (above) makes its way past the limestone caves of Ulu Watu.

A young traveller (left) chats about surfing with a local boy.

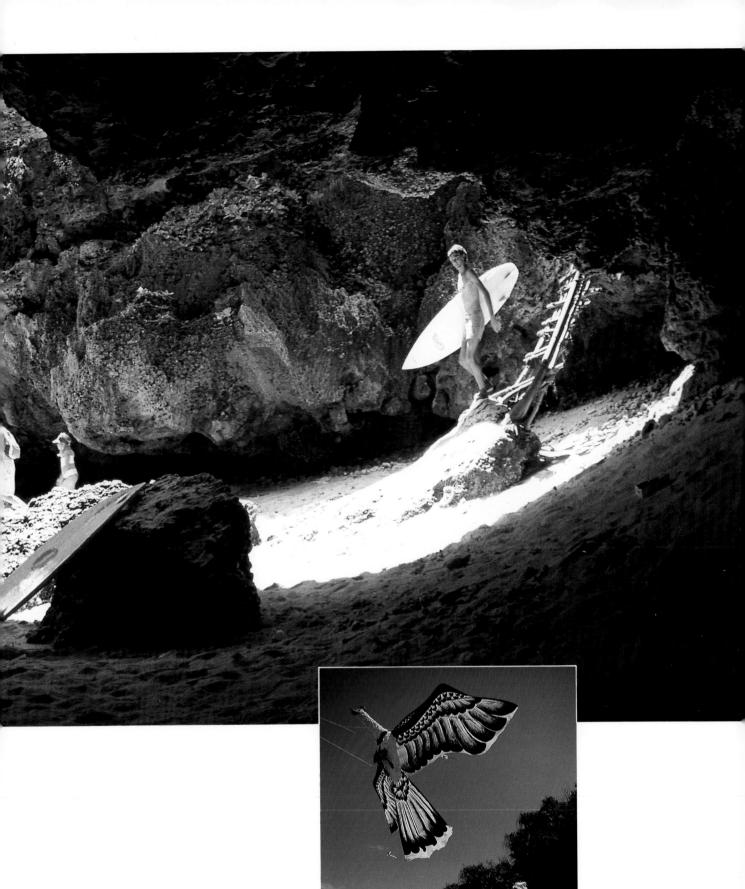

Balinese and tourists alike love the kites and kite festivals along the beaches.

Clouds pile up along the coast
as a solitary walker shares in
the peaceful end of a day.

A boy holds his kite proudly
before letting it soar into the
evening sky.

Following page
A purple sunset descends on
Candi Dasa, an ancient
settlement in Tenganan District,
northeast Bali.

AN A TO Z OF FACTS AND FIGURES

A

Adat This is the traditional law or custom of the land; unwritten, recognized rules of behaviour and conduct covering such matters as taboos, inheritance rights, ownership of land, cooking, eating, courtship, ceremonies of birth, marriage and death, times and methods of sowing rice, the building of houses and praying for rain. *Adat* is the real law of the land, the oldest and most respected.

Agama Hundu Bali Agama Hundu Bali is the official Hindu-Balinese religion.

Airlangga Airlangga was an East Javanese hermit-king who ruled from AD1019—1049 during the 'Golden Age' of Balinese history.

Aling-aling *Aling-aling* is a solid wall behind the entrance gate to a family compound or temple which prevents demons and other malevolent spirits from entering (demons can only travel in straight lines).

Alun-alun *Alun-alun* is the main town square, playing field, and/or town park where public meetings, festivals and sporting events take place. The park-like expanse of lawn usually faces local government offices, post office, banks or schools.

Angklung This portable ensemble is used in many celebrations and processions. Its principal components are rattle instruments, such as hollow bamboo tubes, dating from neolithic times.

Arak A distilled, colourless, fiery palm or rice brandy.

Arja *Arja* is a refined form of folk operetta which utilizes sung dialogue. Themes derive from Hindu, Arabic, Chinese and Balinese sources and usually contain a goodly portion of melodrama and romance sung in Old Javanese meters.

Arjuna Wiwaha A play composed by Mpu Kanwa in AD1035. One of its more famous scenes describes the hero Arjuna meditating in the Himalayas to gain stregth. To test him, Shiva sends heavenly nymphs to dance near him, but his concentration holds.

B

Babad The *babad* (or *gunungan* on Java) means 'the story' and is the triangular symbol of the *wayang* theatre which is set in the middle of the stage when the shadow play begins and ends. It can also be the link that connects the different parts of the play. The *babad* represents the world cosmic order, harmony and peace with nature, and the 'Tree of Life'. Its motions, or the angle at which it is set, reflect the mood of the next scene.

Bale Banjar Headquarters of the village ward; the meeting place of the *banjar* where community events and activities are organized and where *gamelan* rehearse.

Bali Aga Aboriginal, pre-Hindu inhabitants of the non-Javanized villages of Bali, the native 'original' Balinese who resisted the religious and cultural influence of the Javanese Majapahit Empire. Also refers to the religion still practiced in some of the villages of the mountainous northern areas of Bali.

Balian The local witchdoctor, *shaman*, traditional healer, or *dukun* who takes no part in community ritual.

Banjar The local village council, the community extension of the house and family and the basic local political unit.

Bapak Father, headman, leader, male teacher, department head, boss, or a polite way of addressing any older man.

Barong A ferocious but benevolent creature, usually taking the shape of a mythical lion, who battles the evil witch Rangda; it can also refer to the sacred animal mask, worn by two men, with moveable lower jaws, elaborate headdress, twitching tail and long shaggy body.

Barong Dance The most violent and dramatic of Balinese tourist dances. Two demonic characters, Rangda and the Barong, feature in this mythological story. Also called the 'Kris Dance'.

Barong Landung Large, tall puppets representing human-like creatures, supported by a man who carries the puppet's clothing and mask on a wooden frame over his head. This dance play is staged in an annual festival on Serangan Island.

Bemo A small, privately owned, three- or four-wheeled covered pickup truck used for public transport.

Bersih Desa An annual village-cleansing festival which takes place after the harvest to rid a town of evil.

Betel The slightly narcotic nut of the areca palm, chewed with the leaf of the *sirih* vine, *damar* gum and lime paste.

Bharta-yuddha A poetic masterpiece begun by the court poet Mpu Sedah in AD1157. This epic describes a tremendous 18-day battle in Indian mythology between two family groups, the five Pandava brothers (the Five Senses of Man) pitted against hundreds of their evil cousins, the Korawas. The most popular stories and *wayang* figures of today are based directly on this involved Javanized story.

Bima A warrior-lover of the Hundu Mahabharata epic. One of the five Pandava brothers, the biggest and the baddest, this black-headed giant hero is a symbol of superhuman strength and courage.

Bis Malam Special, fast, more expensive buses which travel long distances at night on Java, Bali, South Sulawesi and Sumatra.

Brem Wine made from fermented black rice; tastes a bit like sweet sherry and should be served cold.

Bukit Hill or hilly area; also the name of the arid peninsula separated from southern Bali by a narrow isthmus.

Bupati A local government district officer of one of Bali's eight Kabupaten, appointed by the minister of internal affairs. The Dutch called them 'regents' and governed through them. Their area of jurisdiction is called a 'regency'. In the larger towns the bupati's function can be compared to the position of mayor.

Buta (or bhuta) A demon or obnoxious spirit which can cause sickness or accidents to humans.

C

Candi A Hindu or Buddhist tomb-temple. The term is commonly applied to all ancient monuments and ruins on Java and Sumatra, irrespective of their particular purpose or religion.

Cili A palm-leaf decorative motif, usually the stylized figure of a beautiful young girl. This symbol for wealth and fertility is an important and ubiquitous element of native decorative art.

Copra Coconut meat prised loose from the shell and dried in the sun until it looks like the soles of shoes, curled by the heat and tinged with mould. Coconut oil, which is extracted from it, is used in such products as cooking oil, beauty lotion, soap and nitroglycerin.

D

Dagang Young girls who run refreshment stands in the villages and towns of Bali.

Dalang The *wayang* puppeteer who either manipulates the *wayang kulit* puppets and speaks the words, or narrates the plot for live actors. He is the playwright, producer, director, singer, mystic scholar and poet who jokes, cues the *gamelan*, philosophizes and impersonates.

Dalem (or dalam) Literally 'within', 'deep', or 'inner'. Used to refer to a paramount lord, his residence, his court or his family. The *Pura Dalem*, commonly translated as the 'Temple of Death', is dedicated to Durga, goddess of death, as well as to Dewi Sri, the goddess of rice. Dalem is also the main character, the virtuous king, in *wayang topeng*.

Desa A small, independent agrarian village consisting of a central square, houses, grain–storage sheds, community meeting places, market, temple, *waringin* tree, alarm–drum tower, ricefields, fishponds and forests. Also a general term for rural settlements and their lifestyle, as in *di desa*, 'in the countryside'.

Dewi Sri The goddess of rice and fruits of the earth. From the time of rice-planting to the harvesting, ceremonies are held all over Java and Bali in honour of this old, indigenous, animistic spirit of the rice and of fertility in general.

Dukun Folk doctor, witchdoctor, black–magic advocate, herbalist, druggist, village faith healer, ritual specialist (employing simple prayers or amulets), chronicler, bard, diviner, conjuror or a spiritual leader of great prestige.

Durian The outside of this malodorous fruit is spiked like a mace. The inside consists of three or four compartments where the cream-coloured fruit surrounds large pods. Suck the mushy custard-like pulp from the pod. The taste is indescribable. Tastes like vanilla ice cream with onions, Camembert cheese and nectarines, brandied eggnog with radishes and other such wild combinations. Definitely an acquired taste.

Eka Des Rudra An island-wide purification ceremony which takes place every 100 years, most recently in 1979.

Es Jus A combination of fruit, crushed ice and sweet syrup mixed in a blender. Some spike their *es jus* with liquor.

Gado-gado A Javanese dish of mixed steamed green beans, soy beans, potatoes, cabbage and bean sprouts covered in a rich tangy peanut sauce. Found all over Indonesia.

Galungan Bali's most important cycle of rituals, occurring every 30 weeks, celebrating the new year of the *wuku* or *oton* 210-day calendar. The 10-day Galungan holiday, which celebrates the creation of the universe, is a time of fun, family reunions, prayers and offerings, when the ancestral spirits come down to visit the island for a week.

Garuda A legendary bird that looks like a combination between an eagle and supernatural roc. Garuda, the mount of Vishnu, tried to rescue Sita midflight during her abduction by the devil-king Rawana, but died in the attempt. You see this episode from the *Ramayana* enacted often in *wayang* shows. Garuda is a common motif in Balinese art and the bird is the official modern emblem of the Indonesian Republic. Garuda is also the name of the government-run international airline.

Gringsing A rare *ikat* weaving design, the so-called 'flaming cloth', made only in Tenganan village (Karangasem Regency). Segments of both the warp and the weft threads are bound and dyed before the weaving begins. The gringsing is believed to have magical properties and the ability to protect the wearer from illness.

Halus A term used to describe the most refined cultural traits and behaviour in real life, as well as in characters in the wayang theatre; all gestures, judgements, behaviour or temperaments which are refined, smooth, gracious, pure, polite, noble, subtle, civilized, sophisticated or exquisite.

Ibu Ibu means 'mother'. Also a deferential or affectionate title used when addressing any married woman such as a landlady, washerwoman, or *warung* proprietor. Often used in direct address.

Ider-ider Long narrow, painted cloth friezes in the traditional *wayang* style which are hung along temple eaves.

J_____

Jaba The first (or front or 'outer') temple courtyard or general term for the world outside Bali. Also used to describe the Sudra caste, the fourth caste outside the Triwangsa three caste system. Jaba make up over nine-tenths of Bali's population.

Jaja Multicoloured rice cakes; Balinese 'cookies'.

Jamu Traditional Indonesian herbal medicine made from a mixture of roots, barks and grasses, usually steeped in hot water and drunk. Other *jamu* are applied directly on to the skin, or simply eaten.

Joget (or joged) Social, not religious, dancing. On Bali, this dance form is a socially sanctioned flirtation dance in which a young woman entices boys from the audience to dance with her.

Jukung The Balinese native outrigger sailboat. Often built entirely without metal or nails, a *jukung* incorporates a high level of traditional technology.

Juru Kunci Caretaker and/or 'Keeper of the Shrine'. You must go to this man for the keys to let you into the temple, monument, museum, historical site, etc. A *juru kunci* sometimes produces a guest book and asks for a donation.

Kain Poleng A black-and-white checked cloth used by the Balinese as protective garb against evil influences. Its pattern is believed to convey magic power.

Kaja North, toward the mountain, represented by the colour black and the god Vishnu. A heavenly, lucky and positive direction. All directions in Bali adhere to this compass.

Kala Literally 'badness' or 'evil' but in the figurative sense the demon himself, the son of Shiva and Uma, who invisibly causes evil—a symbol of coarseness and malice. This ground spirit haunts desolate places like the seashores, deep forests and dangerous parts of villages such as the cemetery or the crossroads. A kala-head is the carved stone head of a monster over temple gates and recesses to ward off demonic forces by magic means.

Kasar A term used to describe rough, uncivilized, ungracious, unfit, impolite, coarse or blunt traits in objects, people or skills. Could also mean in poor taste or inappropriate. Includes things like poorly played music, stupid jokes, cheap pieces of cloth or blotchy paintings.

Kawi The classical literary language of early Javanese and Balinese poetry (*kawi* means 'poet'), classical literature and religious texts. Nine out of ten words in it are Sanskrit. This language is very rich, flowery and archaic, well-suited for singing, chanting and musical meter. Kawi is now kept more alive and best preserved on Bali rather than on Java.

Kecak A seated men's choral dance–drama taken from an episode out of the *Ramayana*. Often called the 'monkey dance' because of its characteristic stoccato chorus ('chaka, chaka, chaka'), with the dancers' arms shooting up and bodies contorting like in a voodoo rite. Invented during the 1930s to accompany certain trance dances, today the *kecak* is performed only for tourists.

Kelod South, toward the south, downstream, in the direction of the sea. This direction is demonical, unlucky, negative. It is represented by the colour red and the god Brahma.

Kraton A small walled and fortified palace city. Derived in part from India, the *kraton* was the supreme centre of religious worship in the Hindu-Javanese system of rule.

Kris A double-edged dagger. Designed for thrusting, its blade twists and winds like a snake. Simultaneously a weapon, an ornament, a symbol of masculine strength and the finest example of Balinese metal crafts.

L

Langse Traditional painted tapestries or curtains hung during temple festivals.

Lawar A special food offering made of finely chopped meat, vegetables, grated coconut and other spices, eaten in connection with religious ceremonies and festivals.

Legong A highly stylized classical dance performed by two prepubescent girls.

Leyak A roaming evil spirit or sorcerer that haunts dark, lonely places, roads at night and graveyards. Through knowledge of black magic, these spirits can assume any supernatural shape. They devour the entrails of babies and corpses, cast spells, drink blood from the necks of sleeping people and can manifest as an animal or ball of fire. Rangda is queen of all the *leyak*.

Lingam A Hindu religious symbol in the form of an upright, phallus-shaped, stone column. A lingam is a symbol of virility and manliness, the phallic emblem of Shiva and of male potency. Yoni is the female counterpart.

Losmen Rooms to let. Cheaper than hotels, *losmen* are often family-run inns using traditional native-style structures.

M

Mahabharata A Hindu myth containing 100,000 couplets—the longest epic poem in the world. This is the legend of the descendants of the Hindu gods, reaching its climax in a tremendous 18-day battle between the five Pandava brothers and their cousins, the Korawas, in the mythical state of Bharat during the Vedic Age in India (1500—500BC). The battle makes up less than a quarter of the poem, the remainder consisting of Vedic philosophy, ethics, military science, fairy tales, legendary history, cosmology and the art of statecraft. Translated in the Middle Ages into the high language of Kawi, this Indian masterpiece plays a gigantic part in Balinese literature, art and theatre.

Majapahit An ancient East Javanese empire which held power over much of Indonesia from AD1292—1478, and was finally dissolved by Islamic princes around AD1520. The mightiest indigenous kingdom in Indonesia's history, Majapahit's influence had a profound effect on the art, culture and political organization of Bali.

Melasti This religious procession, a time for casting out evil, takes place the day before Nyepi. Animal sacrifices are made and little boys all over Bali raise general pandemonium to scare away evil spirits.

Mudra Sacred ritual hand gestures, of Hindu or Buddhist origin, that usually accompany mantras in rituals.

N

Naga A Hindu mythical serpent or dragon charged with magic powers. Most snake symbols encountered on Bali are derived from this legendary creature. To augment its power, the blade of the *kris* resembles a *naga*.

Nasi Padang Rice with many side dishes, usually quite spicy-hot. This style of cooking originated in western Sumatra but is now found everywhere in Indonesia.

Ngorod Marriage by elopement in which the bridegroom's friends 'steal' the bride, with her tacit consent.

Nyepi The Balinese New Year according to the Javanese calendar. An annual day of silence, stillness, prayer, meditation and fasting in order to lure evil spirits into thinking that all mankind has deserted the island so that they will also leave. On this day there is no traffic, at night no lamps are permitted and people refrain from all activities.

O

Odalan A temple festival, celebrating the date the temple was founded. Takes place every 210 days, when the gods descend from heaven to receive blessings from the temple congregation. The easiest ceremony to visit on Bali because *odalan* anniversaries follow a fixed and regular schedule.

Oplet A small, covered pickup truck with side benches in the back, used to transport passengers cheaply over short distances. *Oplet* is derived from the Dutch 'to flag down'.

P

Padmasana The high, open seated lotus throne, considered the chief seat of the gods when they descend. Usually located in the northeast corner of a Balinese temple. Dedicated to Surya, the sun-god.

Pagerwesi A festival day during which special offerings are made to ward off any ill-fortune or illness which might strike down the family.

Pak Term of respect for a grown man (from *bapak*, meaning 'father' or 'Mr').

Panca Sila A Sanskrit phrase meaning 'The Five Principles'. This political philosophy was put forth in 1945 by Sukarno to provide a constitutional basis for the Republic. The principles are: belief in one of the four great universal religions; nationalism; Indonesian-style 'guided' democracy; humanitarianism; and a just and prosperous society. Surmounted by a proud eagle, the *Panca Sila* plaque can be seen at the entrance archways of even the smallest villages the width and breadth of Indonesia. These principles are meant to be a point of social and political reference and a touchstone for the state. National education is aimed at producing citizens who are morally responsible to the Five Principles.

Pasanggrahan Government lodge, resthouse or forestry hut which might accept travellers for a modest price or for free.

Pemaksan A voluntary worship group; a congregation responsible for the temple's upkeep and for preparing offerings for the gods.

Pencak Silat The Indonesian national self-defence art, both a lethal fighting skill and a graceful artform.

Plangi A tie-dye technique for decorating cloth practiced in the eastern districts of Bali. In this process the motifs are first drawn or stamped on the fabric, then the figures are sketched in outline by using a tacking thread. When the threads are pulled tight, small loops come up. When the fabric is dipped into the dye vat, the areas that were covered with the string don't absorb the dye, forming a design according to the pattern stitched. Many colours and a broad range of shades can be applied on the one fabric. This technique probably reached Indonesia by way of India.

Pratima Stone figures which portray religious personages. These serve as receptacles or vehicles for deified ancestors or the various manifestations of gods during their visits to Earth.

Pura A terraced temple consisting of three tiers enclosed by walls. A gateway, often lavishly decorated and sculpted, leads to the terraces. The third terrace is usually the most sacred, wherein you find recesses for offerings and shrines. A pura could also be a temporary offering place for invisible deities and ancestors.

Pura Bale Agung The great council temple, dedicated to enhancing the fertility of the land and people.

Pura Dealem 'Temple of the Dead', dedicated to appeasing the spirits of the local uncremated dead. Always situated on the village outskirts in the *kelod* end of the village near the cemetery and the ricefields.

Pura Dea The village– or secular temple used for everyday worship, dedicated to the

82

deities which protect the *desa* in its day-to-day life. Usually located in the middle of the village.

Pura Puseh The temple of origin, the 'navel' temple, dedicated to commemorating the village's first settlers and temple founder. Usually located in the *kaja* end of the village. This temple is the most important social and religious link between the villagers and those of nearby communities that at one time broke away from the mother village.

R

Raksasa A mythical giant from Hindu mythology. Sculptures and reliefs of *raksasa* figures are often seen guarding entrances to temples, erected on either side of the gates. Fierce, moustached, armed with a large club, with long canine teeth sticking out through the cheeks like wild boar's teeth, this demon wards off evil forces.

Ramayana An Indian epic containing 18 books and 24,000 verses divided into 500 songs, all about an Aryan king of the Vedic age. The hero Rama (Vishnu reincarnated) defeats the wicked King Rawana of Ceylon, who has stolen his consort and who is generally troubling the world. This story is known throughout Southeast Asia and all over Indonesia wherever Hindu culture penetrated. The *Ramayana* provides the story line for nearly all Balinese theatre as well as inspiring much of its art, fabric design, painting, sculpture, etc. Written over 2,000 years ago, this epic is as old as Homer's *Iliad* and also incorporated the same legend: the abduction of a great beauty followed by a terrible war to rescue her.

Rangda The famous evil widow, the legendary queen of the witches in Balinese Calon Arang dance–drama. Rangda, who wears an immense, leering, frightening mask, huge white fangs, long sharp nails, flowing hair and out-thrust tongue, is much feared for her very real and dangerous magical power. Yet this old heroine is not entirely evil as she guards the temples and protects the village from demons.

Rejang An ancient ritual purification dance performed only by young unmarried girls, usually in a temple.

S

Sad-kahyangan Special state temples of Bali dedicated to the prosperity of the island and its people as a whole. These important temples include Pura Besakih, Pura Uluwatu, Pura Goa Lawah, Pura Batukau, Pura Pusering Jagat, Pura Kehen, Pura Taman Ayun and Pura Lempuyang Luhur.

Sakti (or *sekti*) Magical or mystical powers; a deity's, animal's or object's spiritual energy or charisma.

Sanghyang A protective deity, a title for a

god. Also ritual dances, the source dance from which a great number of modern-day dances are derived. The most famous and rarest *sanghyang* dance is the *sanghyang dedari* trance dance, the dance of the 'heavenly nymphs', in which two untrained young girls who embody the spirit of deities dance in unison on top of men's shoulders.

Sanghyang Widhi The all-powerful deity in the Balinese religion; the godhead. All Hindu gods and spirits, including Vishnu, Shiva, Brahma and Dewi Sri are manifestations of the cosmic force of Sanghyang Widhi. These ceremonies take place every three Balinese years in the south Bali village of Camangoan (on the way to Gianyar) and Bona (apart from the tourist perfomances there) during the pre-Galungan season.

Saraswati Goddess of learning, science, literature and wisdom, and wife of Brahma. Each *oton* (210 days), elaborate offerings are made and ceremonies held in her honour for books, particularly the sacred *lontar* palm-leaf books. No one is supposed to read on the festival day, Hari Raya Saraswati. Students flock to Pura Jagat Natha in Denpasar.

Sarung (also *sarong*) A *kain* with both ends sewn together, used by men, women and children. Worn with a tight sheathlike effect, the back of the long, loose, tubular-shaped, step-in skirt is folded and tucked in.

Sebel The state of ritual pollution of an individual, family, temple or village. Being spiritually fouled or unclean weakens the spirit of a place or thing.

Sembah Prayer or gesture of reverence to a god or lord superior; a bow with clasped hands.

Songket A fabric with gold or silver weft threads handwoven by the floating-weft technique. *Sarung songket* is traditional wear for high-caste Balinese bridegrooms.

Sudra The term used to designate those Balinese outside the Triwangsa caste system. These 'commoners' are the lowest of Bali's castes and make up about nine-tenths of the population. The term *sudra* is hardly ever used; *Jaba* is much more widely used.

Sunguhu A low-caste priest who performs rituals similar to that of Brahman priests but whose office is limited to the propitiation of evil spirits.

Syahbandar The harbourmaster, found in every port in Indonesia where there are ships. See him about ships and boats to anywhere, when they are expected to arrive or depart and how much you may expect to pay for your passage.

T

Tapel Mask, the Balinese word for *wayang topeng*.

Transmigrasi A government resettlement programme aimed at relocating Javanese and Balinese individuals or communities to the Outer Islands to set up farming colonies under government sponsorship and supervision.

Tukang Artisan, workman, skilled labourer; one who does something (e.g. *tukang banten* is a specialist in preparing offerings.)

V

VOC *Vereenigde Oost-Indische Campagnie*, or United East India Company. A unique Dutch institution established in 1602 by the merger of a number of Dutch trading concerns with the aim of establishing a ruthless monopoly of the spice trade.

W

Warung A poor man's foodstall. It may be a small table, a portable kitchen, or an enclosed structure or building. Many *warung* also sell coffee, soft drinks, cigarettes, canned foods, snacks and *sirih*.

Wayang Kulit Two-dimensional (flat) leather shadow puppets cut out of polished and gilded buffalo leather or goatskin.

Wayang Orang (or *wayang wong*) Traditional live human drama performed on a platform in a theatre with actors and actresses wearing elaborate costume with or without masks (*topeng*). Displaying extrordinary control and discipline, dancers are made up to look like *wayang kulit* puppets, even simulating movements of the shadow figures and relying on the same stylized gestures to convey emotion.

Wayang Topeng Live dance plays in which actors and actresses wear brightly–coloured, expressive wooden masks; up to 80 masks make up one complete set.

Y

Yeh Water, river, waterway or spring (as in *Yeh Sanih*).

Yoni A stylized vagina usually carved out of stone, the Hindu symbol of female life-giving force.

Z

Zirzak Custard apple; with a rich sweet-sour flavour and creamy texture. Though it tastes heavenly, don't overeat as too many will give you a stomach-ache.

INDEX

GS/06/06